K

...IF YOU LIVED IN THE
Alaska Territory

by Nancy Smiler Levinson
Illustrated by Bryn Barnard

SCHOLASTIC INC.
New York   Toronto   London   Auckland   Sydney

CONTENTS

Introduction

Alaska was the forty-ninth state to join the United States. It is the largest state in the nation.

Look at the map and you will see that Alaska lies far to the north of all the other states. It is near the North Pole, at the top of the earth.

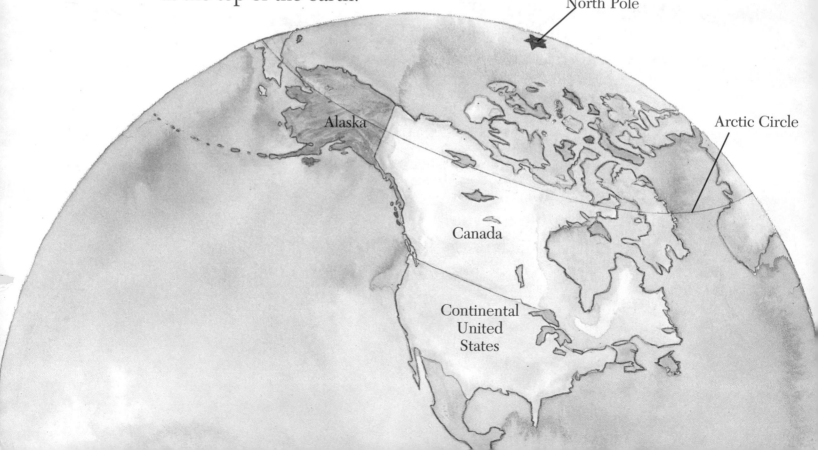

North Pole

Arctic Circle

Alaska

Canada

Continental
United
States

What was the Alaska Territory?

Here is what happened before Alaska became a state:

In 1867, the United States bought Alaska from Russia. In 1912, the U.S. government made Alaska a *territory*.

The Alaska Territory was land that became part of America. All of its people became American citizens. Territory citizens had many of the same rights and privileges as the citizens of the States. But they did not have all of the rights. One thing they could not do was vote for the national president.

Next some people in the territory wanted Alaska to become a state. To become a state, Alaska had to organize its own government first. Here are some steps that the people took to get ready for statehood: They made laws. They elected territory leaders. They created a school system.

Then, after the residents voted for statehood, the U.S. government made Alaska a state. The date was January 3, 1959. (Later that year, the Hawaii Territory became the fiftieth state in the nation.)

This book tells about the Alaska Territory. It tells about the early half of the territory years. Look at the time line. The part that is in color shows that early period — from 1912 to about 1935.

1860	1865	1867	1879	1900	1912	1914-1918	1927	1933	1939–1945	1956	1959	1960

Abraham Lincoln elected President

U.S. buys Alaska from Russia

Thomas Edison invents electric lightbulb

Alaska becomes a U.S. territory

Charles Lindbergh flies across the Atlantic

World War II

Alaska becomes 49th state

Dwight Eisenhower elected President

John F. Kennedy elected President

Andrew Johnson becomes President after Lincoln is assassinated

Early automobiles appear in U.S.

World War I

Franklin Delano Roosevelt elected President

Who lives in Alaska?

Alaskans include many different kinds of people.

They are the Native people, whose ancestors have lived there for thousands of years:
- Eskimo, also called Inupiat and Yupiit
- Aleuts, who live in the Aleutian Islands
- Indians of the Tlingit, Haida, Athabascan, Eyak, and Tsimshian groups.

Alaskans are also many other non-Native people from the United States and other countries who came to Alaska as new settlers.

This book does not tell about all these people. It tells mostly about Eskimo boys and girls, who lived in villages spread across the land. Alaskans call those places far from big towns and roads the Bush.

How to say the Eskimo words

Inupiat say *ih-NOO-pee-AT*
Yupiit say *YOO-peet*
Aleuts say *AL-ee-ootz*
Tlingit say *TLING-git*
Haida say *HI-duh*
Athabascan say *ATH-uh-BASK-un*
Eyak say *EE-yak*
Tsimshian say *TSIM-she-an*

What did people in the United States have at home during Alaska's early territory years?

They had electric lights and radios, but no TVs. They did not have automatic washing machines or dryers. Clothes were hung on a line of rope outside to dry. There were not many refrigerators. People used iceboxes filled with ice chunks to keep food fresh.

Most homes had telephones, but if you wanted to make a long-distance call, you had to ring the operator to make the call for you.

People had hot and cold running water. They bought clothes, food, and furniture from stores.

More and more people bought automobiles. Paved roads began to replace roads of dust and dirt. There were no freeways for them to speed on.

Everywhere in the United States, people liked to travel by train.

Did the early Alaska Territory have the same things?

No. Today, it is easy to reach Alaska by airplane or ship. But long ago, only ships were able to transport goods to Alaska.

Life in the Alaska Territory was very different from life in the States. For almost half the year, much of Alaska is a land of snow, ice, and frozen ground. It is also a land of great waters, islands, wilderness, rain forests, mountains, and volcanoes. Animals and sea life abound there.

Few people in the territory had electricity, a telephone, or hot and cold running water. There were some stores that sold items like dried foods or tools, but the stores were small.

The ancestors of the Native people had gotten everything they needed for food, clothing, and shelter from the land and the sea. Life was hard in that harsh land, but the people had survived there for thousands of years.

The Native people of the early territory got most of what they needed from the land and sea, too. But they were also getting some supplies from outside of Alaska.

Arctic summer
all sun

What are the seasons in Alaska?

Winter, spring, summer, and fall.

Winter is the longest season. It lasts about six months, and it is very, very cold. Rivers and lakes freeze over. Even large parts of the Arctic Ocean freeze over.

On the Arctic coast, temperatures drop to fifty degrees below zero! In the interior region, the climate is dry and cold. Along the southern coast, it is moist and not as cold. In the Panhandle, freezing winds blow fiercely. In the Aleutian Islands, it's rainy, windy, and "pea soup foggy."

Winter in Alaska is dark, too. Our Earth tilts to one side as it orbits around the sun. In winter, the earth's North Pole tilts *away* from the sun.

That means Alaska gets only a few hours of daylight, so the days are short. The closer to the North Pole you live, the fewer hours of light you will have in winter.

Arctic winter
no sun

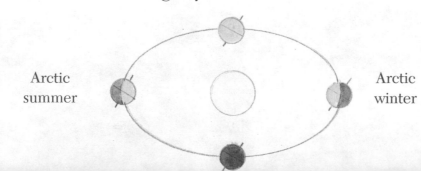

Arctic summer

Arctic winter

Barrow is the closest to the North Pole of any place in Alaska. From November 18 until January 24, it is dark there all night and all day! The sun does not peek above the horizon.

Fall and spring in Alaska are short seasons.

Summer lasts a little longer — from June until September. Mosses, plants, and flowers, such as the arctic primrose, grow wild. In the interior region, it gets warm enough for people to sunbathe and swim.

In summer, days grow extra long. The North Pole tilts *toward* the sun. There are more and more hours of daylight. At Barrow, from May 10 until August 2, the sun never sets.

Sometimes people go out fishing or play baseball at midnight!

Can you imagine living in a land of snow, ice, and frozen earth in a time long ago? Can you imagine long winter months with no daylight when you did not have electricity?

What kind of house would you live in? What kind of clothes would you need? How would you get your food? Would you go to school?

This book will help you imagine Eskimo life if you were a girl or boy in the early Alaska Territory.

What was the most important work of the Eskimo?

The Eskimo have always been great hunters.

In the Alaska Territory, they hunted as their ancestors did. It is their tradition to hunt animals, waterfowl, and fish. They spent most of their time searching for food. Their lives depended on their hunting skills.

At sea, they hunted mammals such as whales, walrus, and seals in the waters of the Pacific and Arctic Oceans, and the Bering Sea.

They hunted waterfowl such as ducks and geese.

On land, they hunted animals such as moose, bears, and caribou. They hunted small game such as rabbits and squirrels, too.

The Eskimo never killed for sport. And they never wasted any part of the animal they killed.

- Animal meat was eaten.
- Skins, or hides, were made into clothing, blankets, sleeping mats, and tents. They were used in making boats and dogsleds.
- Internal organs, such as the intestine, were useful. A seal intestine stretched over a hole in a tent made a good window.
- Blubber (the layer of fat under the skin) of whales, walrus, and seals was eaten, too. Blubber also was melted into oil and burned for heat and light in lamps made of soapstone (soft rock).

• Sinew (part of the muscle) was dried and twisted into thread and fishing lines.

• Bones were used to make frames for boats and dogsleds. The Eskimo invented hunting weapons and cutting tools made out of bone. A small bone of a bird made a fine sewing needle.

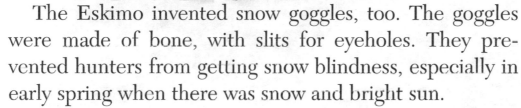

The Eskimo invented snow goggles, too. The goggles were made of bone, with slits for eyeholes. They prevented hunters from getting snow blindness, especially in early spring when there was snow and bright sun.

The bright glare of sunlight on the snow could burn a person's eyeballs — like you get sunburn on your skin. That is snow blindness.

Snow blindness can cause a problem in seeing different colors. Or it can cause the eyes to water or feel scratchy. The problem can last for many days.

If a hunter had snow blindness, he might have to go many days without hunting food for his family.

Hunting was work that never ended.

What weapons did people use to hunt?

The Eskimo hunted the same ways their ancestors had. They used spears, harpoons, and bows and arrows.

In the territory years, some Eskimo also used guns. Guns had been brought to Alaska by explorers and fur traders before Alaska became a territory.

How did people hunt at sea?

Men and boys hunted on the open sea in two kinds of boats.

One was an *umiak*, a long, deep boat made of sealskin tightly pulled over a frame of whalebone or driftwood. Several people fit in the umiak and paddled with oars.

The second boat was a *kayak*, a small sealskin canoe for one person. The person fit snugly inside a small opening. He steered with a paddle that had a blade at each end.

How to say the Eskimo words

umiak   say *OO-mee-ak*
kayak   say *KI-ak*

It would take many lessons for a boy to learn to use a kayak.

First he would learn about the directions of the wind and the ocean currents. Then he would be taught how to balance himself getting in and out of the boat.

Next he would practice paddling and then learn how to stay inside the kayak when big waves flipped the boat over.

Finally he would learn to control the boat while harpooning or shooting a walrus or seal at the same time.

Often he would have to wait hours alone on the rolling sea before he could make a kill. Learning to be patient was an important lesson for every Eskimo boy.

How did hunters travel over frozen land and ice?

Sleds brought hunters long distances over ice and frozen ground.

The sleds were pulled by huskies. These dogs have a heavy coat of fur and can survive in very cold weather. Most of the time they sleep outside.

The frames of the sleds were made of pieces of whale-bone or driftwood. The pieces were laced together with strips of animal hide.

If whalebone or wood were not available, sometimes people used whole frozen fish as slats stretched across the surface of the sled.

The sled runners were coated with mud and moss, which would freeze, so the runners would glide easily on the snow.

A good dog team would have ten or twelve dogs. The loads they pulled were very heavy. Hunters' gear — a tent, lamps and oil, tools, fur blankets, and food for men and the dogs — could weigh as much as eight or nine hundred pounds.

Dogs were the only tamed animals in Alaska. But they were not pets for your family. Huskies had to be firmly raised and trained so they could perform the hard job of pulling sleds for days at a time.

What kind of house would you live in?

There were different kinds of houses. Many families lived in one kind of house in the winter and another kind in the summer.

An Eskimo winter house was just like the ones their ancestors had lived in. It was a one-room house that was built partly underground.

A deep space was dug into the earth and framed inside with driftwood or whalebone. The opening was framed, too, and then covered with animal skins. Clumps of dried sod (topsoil), bundles of grass, and layers of stone were packed on top of the skins.

You entered by crawling through a tunnel that led into the room. The tunnel, which was lower than the room, trapped cold air and kept it out of the living space. At the same time, warm air was trapped inside and could not escape. You would be so warm and snug that you would not need to wear clothes in your house.

Inside, there were no tables or chairs. There were sleeping platforms covered with animal skins or mats. Clothes and fishing equipment hung on wall pegs.

There was no bathroom or running water. Buckets were used instead of toilets. They were called "honey buckets," and they were emptied outside.

People used an oil lamp for light, for cooking, and to melt snow into water for drinking. The lamp was made of soapstone and was filled with blubber and a moss wick. Moss plants were picked in summer and saved. When the wick was lit, a fire could burn for days without going out.

In the summer, people moved two or three times to different outdoor fishing and hunting camps.

Then you would need a house that was easy to put up and take down. The best kind was an animal-skin tent, supported by wood or bone poles. It would have a doorway, a window of transparent seal intestine to let in light, and a smoke hole at the top.

Were there other kinds of houses?

Settlers built log cabins and wood-framed houses with four or five rooms and glass windows. There was a separate outhouse for the toilet.

These kinds of houses were new to the Eskimo, but in the later territory years, Native people lived in them, too.

Before electricity came to Alaska, people in log cabins and wood-framed houses cooked on a wood-burning stove. They got their light from a kerosene fuel lantern. Lanterns don't give off light as well as electric lamps.

What did people do at home in the evenings? They sewed, made carvings, repaired tools, and told stories.

Or they might do what other people around the world did on dark winter nights before they had electricity: Go to sleep early!

Would you ever live in an igloo made of snow?

No. In Alaska you would *not* live in a snow igloo. They were used by the Eskimo of Canada and Greenland.

The Eskimo word *iglu* means shelter. A snow house is one kind of shelter.

How to say the Eskimo word

iglu   say *IG-loo*

The people in Canada and Greenland didn't live in snow shelters all winter long. They used them for a few nights while traveling or hunting with a team of sled dogs.

They cut big blocks of packed snow and built them into a dome-shaped house. The entrance was a low tunnel. The tunnel kept out the cold air and snow. The tunnel was also a good place for the dogs to sleep.

The snow house was ventilated for air to circulate and insulated with warm air at the same time!

A soapstone and oil lamp gave light and extra heat. If a wall dripped, a small roof opening was made for added ventilation, and the drip would freeze over fast.

What food did people eat?

Eskimo ate mainly fish and meat.

There were fish such as salmon, grayling, pike, herring, cod, halibut, and trout.

Meat came from animals such as whales, walrus, seals, and caribou. An important meal was *maktak,* which is the inner layer of whale skin with a thick layer of blubber beneath it.

You could eat your meat raw, raw frozen, or cooked. Any way you ate it, you would get all the vitamins and nutrition you needed.

In the summer, you could add fowl such as ducks or geese to your menu. And berries. Lots of berries! Cranberries, blueberries, crowberries, salmonberries, and cloudberries. The berries were an important source of vitamin C.

How to say the Eskimo word

maktak   say *MUCK-tuck*

And for dessert? How about Eskimo ice cream? Here is how you make it: First you get some seal oil or caribou fat. Add berries and sugar. Maybe a little boiled fish. Whip it all together.

It tastes delicious!

How would you keep the food fresh?

You would not need a refrigerator in the winter! There were plenty of other ways to preserve food for freshness or for hard times when food supplies might get low.

Eskimo families in the Bush buried meat under their houses in a deep layer of earth called permafrost. Since permafrost is always frozen, it was like storing meat in a freezer.

Nastasia Keene and her family collected berries in woven sacks. After they tied the sacks tightly, they put them in a lake that froze over. In the middle of winter they chopped the ice and took out the sacks. Nastasia found the berries "very fresh and very good."

Many Alaskans preserved fish by smoking them in wood-burning stoves and hanging them on racks to dry. The Eskimo preserved salmon by beating the fish, scoring the skins with knives, and hanging them on wooden racks to dry in the air.

On the Aleutian Island of Afognak, a mother saved dried fish skins for her family. When there wasn't enough food that winter, she dug up the skins and toasted them. "How good they were when we were hungry!" her children remembered.

Part 1 ③

What language did the Eskimo speak?

There are four related Eskimo languages spoken in Alaska. They are: Inupiaq, Siberian Yupik, Central Alaskan Yupik, and Alutiiq.

The Eskimo use many different kinds of words to talk about weather, hunting, fishing, and animals.

We use many words to describe the many forms of ice and snow. The Eskimo have a special word for each of these forms.

Here are some Inupiaq snow and ice words:

Eskimo word	English meaning
aniu (say *un-EE-oo*)	general term for snow
qannik (say *KON-neek*)	snowflake
qanniksuq (say *KON-necks-uk*)	it is snowing
natiġviksuq (say *nu-TUR-veeks-uk*)	snow is drifting, blowing along the ground
apun (say *UH-pon*)	snow cover on the ground
nutaġaq (say *NOO-tu-ak*)	fresh, powder snow
pukak (say *POOK-uk*)	sugar snow (granular)
siḷḷiq (say (*SEEL-lie-k*)	hard crusty snow
apuyyaq (say *uh-POO-ee-yak*)	patch of snow
siku (say *SEE-koo*)	ice
kusulugaq (say *koo-SOO-loo-gak*)	icicle
muġaliq (say *MUH-ruh-lick*)	slush ice
qinu (say *KEY-noo*)	broken chunks of slush ice
sarri (say *SIR-ree*)	pack ice
puktaaq (say *pook-TAK*)	iceberg

Would you live in a town?

Most Eskimo lived in a village. If you lived in a village, people would say that you were "out in the Bush."

Villages were near water, either by an ocean, a river, or a bay, so that people could hunt and fish.

Some were tiny groups of about ten people. Others were larger. If you lived in a larger village, you would have had two or three hundred neighbors.

There were no roads between villages. There were no roads inside a village, either. People made their own foot-paths or sled paths to get from place to place.

Villages such as Koyukuk or Scammon Bay had a church, several barns, a graveyard, a jail, a one-room schoolhouse, and a social hall for people to meet. There might be one small store, too.

Maybe there was one telephone at the store for the whole village to use. Some communities had a shortwave radio that was linked to other communities in case of an emergency.

The store sold things such as flour, sugar, tea, dried or canned fruit, tools, pots, and pans.

Many things had to come by ship from the lower forty-eight states or from another country. Each shipment took months at a time to arrive, so there were only a few deliveries a year.

You would cheer when the first supply of goods arrived in spring after breakup (when ice broke up) — especially if you got a treat like chewing gum or a fresh apple or orange!

Did Alaska have cities?

About five or six cities came into being during the territory years.

Many non-Native people lived and worked in the cities. Eskimo and Aleuts, as well as Tlingit, Haida, Athabascan, Eyak, and Tsimshian groups, lived and worked there, too.

The largest cities, Anchorage and Juneau, had populations of about four or five thousand people.

A city had wood-framed houses, horse stables, and a few small hotels. There was a barbershop and a bank.

You could get your picture taken in a photography studio. You could go to a live musical show on a theater stage.

Every city had at least one school. In Fairbanks, the schoolhouse was painted red. It was two stories high. Grammar-school pupils were divided into grades downstairs. High-school classes were held upstairs.

Alaska was still a wilderness full of wild animals. At recess in the Fairbanks school, a moose might wander onto the playground. Then recess would be cut short.

Every city had a "main street" that was a very wide road. Dog teams and carriages had plenty of room to drive. After all, there was plenty of wide-open space in all of Alaska!

During the early territory years, the government set to work building a railroad line. The trains ran between the cities of Seward and Fairbanks and passed through Anchorage. (That railroad still runs today.)

If you moved from the Bush to a city you might find it crowded and noisy at first. You might even find the change a big shock!

What would your family life be like?

You slept and ate with your family. You worked together every day. Everyone needed to help out so that families could survive in the Alaskan Bush.

You and your family were together nearly all the time.

What did fathers do? They hunted and provided food and shelter. They took care of the hunting weapons, the dogs and the dogsled, and the boat they used to hunt at sea.

What did mothers do? They took care of the children. They cooked, gathered plant food, and stored them, too. They sewed clothes for the whole family and skin covers for the boats.

Boys and girls did chores such as hauling water, fishing, and looking after their younger brothers and sisters.

Adults taught children skills to survive that were not explained in books. Lessons from the elders gave the children an important traditional education.

Girls and boys were taught different tasks.

Girls learned to sew and mend clothes and to scale, wash, and cook fish. They learned to use the *uluaq*, or *ulu*, a knife with a curved blade and a wooden handle. It was called a woman's knife because women used it to cut fish, cut skins for clothing, and chop ice.

Boys were taught to fish and hunt. At age twelve they learned to go out to sea in a kayak. At fourteen they were

How to say the Eskimo words

uluaq   say *OO-loo-ak*
ulu   say *OO-loo*

expected to kill their first seal and share the meat with the community.

They were also taught to avoid dangers such as drowning, freezing, starving, and being attacked by a bear or wolf.

One boy, Paul Tiulana, lived on King Island in the Bering Sea. His brother and uncle made him a small "practice" harpoon and bow and arrow. To help strengthen his body, they had him walk for hours across the ice without stopping.

"If we did not learn to hunt and to survive out on the ice," said Paul, "we would be dead."

Did families go fishing together?

In the spring, families scattered to outdoor camps near rivers and lakes or along the coast where fish were plentiful.

Your family might go to a salmon camp. Boys and girls would help catch fish with a net, basket trap, or spear. Then they would help smoke and dry the fish to preserve it.

Some children might set traps for porcupines, squirrels, and foxes. Or dig roots of "chocolate lilies," the roots of brown-flowered plants that were tasty when they were boiled.

When the summer was over and people returned to their winter houses, they did not let frozen rivers and lakes stop them from fishing.

Toward the end of winter your family's supply of stored fish would be gone. Then you would need to go fishing through the ice.

At Scammon Bay you would go out to a shallow river or creek and cut a hole in the ice with a heavy ice pick.

If you were fishing for needlefish, you would use a net. For tomcods, instead of using live bait, you would use a line with a shell.

People also used chicken-wire traps, which were pushed into the muddy bottom of the river or creek. You might find a few drowned muskrats in the trap along with the fish. Their skins would make a good pair of mittens.

Your family would be glad to have your ice catch at the end of the winter.

Did families have time for fun?

Picnics were fun. So were sledding and tobogganing!

If you didn't have a sled, you might use an animal skin to slide down a snow mound. Polar bear skins were cleaned this way. But if you used a caribou or seal skin, your mother would scold you. Those skins were needed for clothes and tents. They were not to be wasted!

In a social hall you could play games or, on a rare occasion, join in a village dance with a musician who played a fiddle or accordian. Sometimes a village got to see a movie that had been sent by ship.

Families liked storytelling, especially on long winter nights. You might have listened to a story like "How the Raven Stole the Stars, the Moon, and the Sun." Or a true story about how your great-grandfather escaped a polar bear attack.

What clothes would you wear?

You would need special clothes for the winter. Without them, you could not survive.

You would wear a long parka with a hood, pants, mittens, and boots. They would all come from animals.

A good skin for a parka and pants was caribou, because it is waterproof. Parkas and pants were kept closed by drawstrings. They had no zippers or snaps. They had no buttons or buttonholes for the wind to whistle through.

The fur trim on the parka hood was called a *ruff*. The best trim is made of wolverine fur. Wolverine hairs don't freeze because they are hollow, so you wouldn't have iced-up fur around your face.

You would also wear winter underwear. That's another set of skins, like fox, that you put on underneath your warm outside clothes. You would wear this inside layer with the fur side of the animal facing your skin.

Eskimo call their boots *kamiks*. They came up to your knees. They were made of sealskin and were waterproof, too. Inside you would wear rabbit-skin stockings. You would also stuff in bunches of dried grass for extra insulation and warmth.

How to say the Eskimo word

kamiks   say *KUH-micks*

What did babies wear?

Babies were carried nearly naked on their mothers' backs, inside their mothers' warm parkas. The babies wore diapers made of clumps of moss held on by pieces of animal skin.

The only part of a baby that showed was its head, and that was covered by a little fur hood.

A baby was supported underneath by a pouch that was tied around its mother's body.

When a child was old enough to walk, it was dressed in a small one-piece suit and a little pair of boots.

How were the clothes made?

The women worked hard at making clothes. They spent almost every day of the fall and much of the winter at this work.

They stripped, cut, dried, and scraped the animal skins. Then they softened the pieces by chewing them. Hands and teeth were important tools.

Next they sewed the pieces together. They used a needle made of bird bone, or sometimes steel, and thread made from long, twisted strands of animal sinew.

The women had to take special care at this task. All the pieces had to be sewn together tightly to keep air, moisture, and wind out.

But at the same time, the clothes needed to fit loosely on the body. So, there would be a layer of air between your skin and your clothes. The layer of air acts as an insulator to keep you warm.

If your clothes were too tight, you would sweat. Sweat draws out the layer of air between your skin and clothes. Without that air, you would freeze to death.

How would you take care of your clothes?

You had to take extra-special care of your clothes.

Each time you entered the tunnel of your house, you would remove your outer clothes and beat off the snow crystals with a curved, flat, wooden snow-beater called a *tiluktuun*.

Then you would hang your clothes on pegs to dry.

If you didn't, your clothes would end up as stiff as a log!

How to say the Eskimo word

tiluktuun   say *tee-luke-TOON*

Would you go to school?

Many Eskimo children began going to an American-style school for the first time when Alaska became a territory.

A newly built village school was a wood-frame building with one or possibly two rooms. A school bell hung from a rope outside.

Inside, there were a row of handmade wooden seats, a table and a few chairs, a small blackboard with chalk, and some old books. The room was heated by a potbellied stove.

Teachers were newcomers to the Alaska Territory. In the village of Kulukak, the teacher came from the state of Washington. The schoolroom was connected to her house. Her name was Mrs. Madenwald, but the pupils called her *Skuularista*. (It sounds like *School*arista).

If you were in her class, you would sit with twenty other pupils. Some were five years old. Some were fifteen. One was a grandmother who wanted to learn to read and write, too.

The new pupils felt shy the first day. You might have felt shy, too. But Skuularista would make hot chocolate for everyone. You would all begin to feel better.

Sometimes teachers were not only teachers. They might also be nurses or barbers!

They would give you an aspirin and a tonic medicine for a cough. They would cover a scraped knee with a Band-Aid from their first-aid kits. If your mother gave permission, your teacher might give you a haircut, too.

What would you learn in school?

In the village schools, you would learn to say the Pledge of Allegiance to the American flag and to sing "My Country 'Tis of Thee."

You would memorize and recite the letters of the alphabet, spelling words, and arithmetic sums.

You would read Mother Goose rhymes and stories about children who were well-behaved. You would have social studies lessons about important people in American history such as George Washington and Abraham Lincoln. You would also learn rules for good health care.

Sometimes girls learned cooking and sewing. Boys might work at carving and crafts.

In territory schools, children also learned the English language, which was very different from their Eskimo tongue.

What was school like for Eskimo children?

It was hard at first.

If you had never been to school before, it would be a strange, new place to you.

Besides, if you lived in a tiny village with no school, you might be sent to a village that had one. Then you would have to leave your family for many months at a time. You would live with other people who were strangers to you. Learning to speak the English language was hard because Eskimo children were often forbidden to speak their own language in school.

Some United States government people hoped to make boys and girls "more American" by forcing them to "forget" their Native tongue.

It was also hard learning to read English because the reading lessons were all about people and places around the world that Eskimo boys and girls had never heard of.

Suppose you had never been outside of your village.

You had never heard a radio. You had never seen a newspaper or books with pictures.

Now suppose you are a new pupil in an Alaska Territory school. You might have a reading lesson about big-city skyscrapers or about a farmer milking cows.

Would it be hard learning to read those lessons? Can you think why?

Some teachers had a good idea to help their pupils learn to read. The teachers and the children made their own picture storybooks.

Here are some of their stories:

• Wassily trapped a red fox. He will take it to the trading post.

• Chunook has a new parka. Her mother and Ocalena made it for her.

• The reindeer herd is near the village. We like to eat reindeer meat.

If you were a new Eskimo pupil in the Alaska Territory, would you learn to read English more easily with those stories? Can you think why?

What games would you play?

One favorite game was bull-roarer. You would tie a string to a thin blade of wood or bone and swing it fast over your head like a propeller. That would make a loud, whizzing, bull-roaring noise. Maybe you could make a louder whiz than your friends!

Another game was making string figures by looping string over and around your fingers.

Boys played with small bone or ivory carved animals. Girls played with carved dolls that were dressed in tiny parkas, mittens, and boots just like their own clothes.

Games such as tug-of-war, kickball, and wrestling were popular.

Blanket toss was popular, too. People stood in a circle, holding the edges of stretched walrus skins. It was like a trampoline. You would stand in the center and get bounced five feet! Ten feet! Fifteen feet into the air!

Eskimo hunters tossed each other like that so they could spot animals in the distance to hunt. That's how the game of blanket toss began.

What if you got sick?

If people got very sick or had an accident out in the Bush, it would be almost impossible to get to a hospital.

Villages had no doctors, but a few had a small public health clinic. There was usually one medical aide who did simple things such as stopping a nosebleed or offering a spoonful of medicine.

Even though Alaskans knew about some new ways to heal, many still used older, traditional methods at home. If your stomach ached, your mother might rub seal oil on your belly.

In January 1925, two children in the town of Nome got very sick and died from a disease called diphtheria. That deadly disease spreads and kills quickly unless treated with a special serum (medicine). Everyone wanted to stop the disease, but there was not enough serum in Nome.

A doctor tapped out a radiotelegraph message. A hospital in Anchorage, nearly 800 miles away, responded.

Yes, they said, they had a supply of serum. But it would take two or three weeks to get to Nome.

They sent the serum by train to the end of the railroad line. Then a relay of dog teams took over for the longest part of the journey — 658 miles.

The dogs and sled drivers rode day and night through blizzards, below-zero temperatures, and across dangerous ice floes.

Finally the last relay team arrived in Nome. The serum was delivered after a journey of only five-and-a-half days! The town of Nome was saved.

How did people get mail?

Mail was often delivered by dogsled, but it was not delivered very often.

First the mail arrived in the Alaska Territory by ship. A dog team and drivers met the ship at the port and loaded mailbags onto the sled.

Then the dogsled journey began — up rivers, down creeks, and across woods, stopping at village after village.

In the winter, the sled traveled swiftly over ice and snow. The journey would take several days.

But in places where the ice had thawed, the sled often had to be pushed over the bare ground trail. That journey might take two or three weeks.

At last the mailman would arrive at your village. Everybody would be happy to see him!

People were so happy that sometimes they held a dance. The mailman was the guest of honor!

What Native Alaskan festivals did people celebrate?

They celebrated important seasonal events, such as the time of "getting ready to hunt" in the fall.

Village members sang and danced as one person beat a drum called a *qilaun*. The qilaun was a flat, one-sided drum made of animal intestine or bladder stretched over a round wood frame.

Sometimes people danced while they wore masks carved to look like animals or birds. That was the Eskimo way of honoring those living creatures of the land and sea.

If the men in your village returned from a successful whale hunt, then everyone would celebrate to give thanks for getting food for the winter.

One of the most important Eskimo celebrations was the Messenger Feast. This took place when people of one community invited members of another community to join them for food, games, dancing, and an exchange of gifts.

How to say the Eskimo word

qilaun   say *KEE-lawn*

The Messenger Feast was a time for communities to strengthen bonds of friendship with one another. Friendship, too, is a treasured gift.

What United States holidays did people celebrate?

You would celebrate almost all the holidays that you do now.

Adults even gave parties on election days after citizens of the territory voted a governor or a judge into office.

The biggest celebrations took place on Thanksgiving, Christmas, and the Fourth of July.

Alaska did not have turkeys to serve on Thanksgiving. Instead, you might share a big reindeer meat dinner with village neighbors.

At Christmas, girls and boys decorated their classrooms with chains of brightly painted mussel shells and pictures of Santa Claus. Sometimes they put on a holiday show for the community.

Many boys and girls received Christmas gifts from the American Junior Red Cross in the lower forty-eight states.

Handkerchiefs and socks were useful gifts. But the best kind of surprises were balloons, Cracker Jack, and taffy candy.

Independence Day is an American holiday honoring the independence and freedom of the nation. It is celebrated on July 4th.

If you lived on St. Lawrence Island, you would celebrate Independence Day all day long with your family and neighbors.

In the morning, everyone would meet at the school flagpole and salute the flag. Throughout the day, fathers took part in shooting skill contests and boat races. Boys and girls joined in footraces and peanut tosses. There was a picnic supper and then a dance.

The Fourth of July was a most exciting day to celebrate!

Afterword

Life for the Eskimo in Alaska began to change rapidly during the last half of the territory years (from about 1936 to 1959).

More and more things arrived in the territory. Some new things were:

- Snowmobiles and powerboats for hunters and fishermen
- Many kinds of guns
- Radios and TVs
- Telephones
- Sewing machines
- Machine-made clothes such as shirts, dresses, and blue jeans

Some new methods of transportation were:

- A railroad that connected Fairbanks to Anchorage and Seward
- Automobiles
- Small airplanes

Some new foods that the Eskimo added to their diet were:

- Milk
- Macaroni
- Peanut butter sandwiches
- Salmon preserved in cans

Now the people:

- Wear animal-skin parkas and machine-made jackets
- Travel by dogsled and snowmobile
- Get food from hunting and from opening a can
- Eat both maktak and macaroni
- Speak Eskimo and English languages

Many people say that the Eskimo are "caught between two worlds."

The first is the traditional world of their ancestors, living off the land and the sea. That is called a subsistence lifestyle.

The second is the world of machines and the many modern ways of Western civilization.

Some people like living in two worlds. They believe that modern ways make their hard lives easier and more comfortable.

One woman, Mary Ann Sundown, says: "I like the life we used to live long ago, but we were always in need of something. We live in comfort now. I don't go hungry. Both lives are good. I like both."

Other people do not like living in two worlds. They know that machines and medicine can be helpful, but they worry that old Eskimo ways will disappear forever.

One man, Pete Abrams, says: "In the old days, our people knew how to survive on the ocean and on land. Now we're spoiled with things like running water and telephones. We're not using our minds and bodies to survive."

Pete wants his children to know about their heritage. He is teaching them the language of their ancestors, and he tells them stories of their people long ago. He hopes that his children will pass on the language and stories to their children.

The Eskimo have survived in the far north for a long, long time. Now they hope to survive the many changes in Alaska and to be able to live successfully in both worlds.

For Linda Burns and Dick Burns, who have always been willing to share
—NSL

For Parks —BB

Author's acknowledgments

I would like to thank the following for their assistance in the research and writing of this book:
Lawrence Kaplan, Ph.D., Alaska Native Language Center, University of Alaska, Fairbanks;
Nancy Warren Ferrell, Juneau; Jim Fox, Palmer; Air Force Sgt. Richard Hamilton, Supervisor, Arctic
Survival School, U.S. Air Force, Fairbanks; Gladi Kulp, Alaska Division of State Libraries, Juneau;
Pattey Parker, Alaska Geographical Society; Katherine and John Parker, Anchorage.

Abbie Morgan Madenwald's book, *Arctic Schoolteacher, 1931–1933*, was particularly helpful
in the preparation of this manuscript, as was Nancy Warren Ferrell's book, *Alaska, A Land in
Motion,* produced through the cooperation of the Alaska Department of Education; the University
of Alaska, Fairbanks, Department of Geography; and the Alaska Geographic Alliance.

I am also especially grateful to my editor, Eva Moore.

ISBN 0-590-74449-6

12 11 10 9 8 7 6 5 4   1 2 3/0

Printed in the U.S.A.   08
First Scholastic printing, February 1998

Book design by Laurie Williams